Bible Stories Activities

Moses

MW01047556

6412 Maple Ave.
Westminster, CA 92683
ISBN: 978-1-4206-7903-8
©2008 Learning Train
Made in U.S.A.

Table of Contents

Introduction

Most children who go to Sunday school know quite a bit about Moses. The story of his birth and the unique way his mother kept him safe is told to preschoolers to show how God cares for His children. The story of Moses leading his people out of Egypt and across the Red Sea is a favorite that reminds children of God's power and our need to trust Him. Then, of course, Moses is the one to whom God gave the Ten Commandments up on Mount Sinai, and his trust in God is an example to us all. However, we also discover in the wilderness wanderings of Moses and his people on the way to Canaan that he had an ungovernable temper which resulted in his not being able to enter the Promised Land.

The stories and activities in this book cover the most popular stories about Moses and some of the not-so-well-known ones from his birth to his death. Students will enjoy learning about him through word search puzzles and crosswords, crafts, action rhymes and songs, a skit, and a variety of other fun, creative activities. Most activities requre that they use their Bibles to find answers or to check their answers. A complete answer key is provided on pages 47–48 for your convenience.

The book is divided into 11 stories of Moses with correlated activities: his birth, leaving Egypt after killing an Egyptian, hearing from God through a burning bush, going back to Egypt to confront Pharaoh, facing Pharaoh and warning him of the ten plagues of God, directing his people to keep the first Passover, leading the people out of Egypt, parting the Red Sea, wandering for 40 years in the desert, receiving the Ten Commandments from God, building the tabernacle, and dying without ever entering the Promised Land. A bulletin board is provided on pages 4–5 and can be used throughout the study of Moses. Some of the pages are all about Moses while others are application activities to help students look at their own relationships with God and other people and discover what God wants them to do. The stories of Moses' life were included in the Bible not just to inform us about one of God's great leaders; but to help us learn important truths from his successes and failures. Be sure to take time to make sure students understand each story and see how it applies to their everyday lives.

The last words in the book of Deuteronomy describe Moses: "Since then no prophet has risen in Israel like Moses, whom the LORD knew face to face, who did all those miraculous signs and wonders the LORD sent him to do in Egypt—to Pharaoh and to all his officials and to his whole land. For no one has ever shown the mighty power or performed the awesome deeds that Moses did in the sight of all Israel." (Deuteronomy 34:10–12) Moses' life demonstrates that God chooses to use imperfect people to do His will. In him we see how God can use His strength to transform our weaknesses!

Moses Bulletin Board

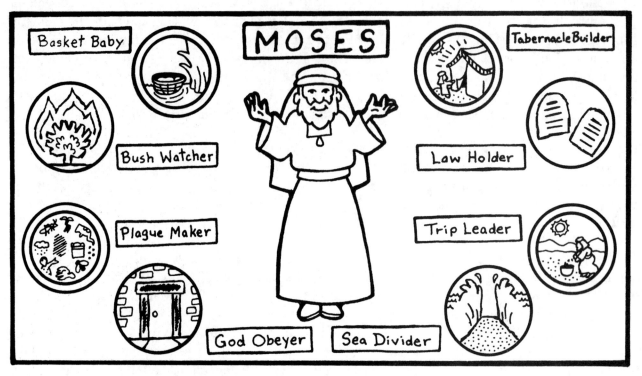

1. Cover the bulletin board with light yellow paper.

2. Copy the patterns on page 5. Color them and cut them out.

3. Cut out eight large circles from light colored construction paper.

4. Cut Moses' name from construction paper or print it on paper and mount it at the top of the board.

5. Mount the adult figure of Moses on the center of the board.

6. Arrange the eight circles around the board.

7. Cut out eight or more construction paper name strips and attach them to the board.

8. After each of the following stories of Moses, mount the appropriate picture on a circle or draw one as instructed:

   • Baby Moses—baby in basket (page 5)

   • Burning Bush—draw a burning bush

   • Ten Plagues—plague art (page 5)

   • First Passover—draw a door post with blood over it

   • Crossing the Red Sea—draw water

   • In the Desert—manna (page 5)

   • Ten Commandments—draw two stone tablets

   • Building the Tabernacle—tabernacle (page 5)

9. Have children suggest titles for Moses to go along with each story. Print them on the name strips on the board. (See the suggestions on the board above.)

Moses Bulletin Board

Bulletin Board Patterns

Baby Moses

(Based on Exodus 1:1–2:10)

When Joseph's family came to live with Joseph in Egypt, there were 70 of them. Over the years the families grew and had more and more children. About 350 years later, there were over two million Jews (called Hebrews in the first chapters of Exodus) living in the idol-worshiping land of Egypt. The Pharaoh, who had been kind to Joseph's family, had long since died and other leaders had taken his place. Now a new Pharaoh ruled Egypt and he had bad feelings toward the Jews. In fact, he wanted to get rid of them. He was nervous about having so many non-Egyptians in the land. If Egypt went to war, would the Jews turn against Egyptians and fight for the enemy? How could he handle so many "foreigners" in his country?

Pharaoh's solution to the problem was to make all the Jewish people serve as slaves. He appointed slave masters over them and worked them so hard, many of them died building huge structures for the Egyptian government. They were treated cruelly, but instead of the Jewish population going down, it continued to increase. The Jewish midwives who assisted women when they gave birth were told to kill any newborn boy babies. However, the midwives feared God and did not obey these orders. They excused themselves by saying that Jewish women gave birth so quickly, it was usually all over before the midwives got there. Finally, Pharaoh gave orders to all his people to throw all boy infants into the Nile River to drown. Girl babies could be kept alive.

It was during this troubling time that a Jewish couple, Amram and his wife Jochebed, had a baby boy. Amazingly, they were able to keep his birth a secret for three months, but Jochebed finally decided she had to do something to protect her son. She coated a grass basket to make it waterproof; then she laid her baby boy in it and put a cover on it. She took the covered basket down to the river and set it in the water among the tall reeds by the riverbank. Then she went home, trusting God to take care of her child when she could not. Her daughter Miriam stayed some distance away to see what would happen to her little brother.

The Bible does not say how long the basket was in the water, but what happened to it was surely from the hand of God. Pharaoh's daughter went down to the river to bathe and saw the basket. She sent one of her attendants to get it and bring it to her. When she opened the basket she saw the crying baby and she felt sorry for him. She recognized that he was a Jewish baby and knew what she should do with him. Would she have had him thrown into the river if she had taken time to think about it? Who knows? God sent Miriam along at just the right time. The girl walked up to the princess and offered to get a Jewish woman to nurse the baby for her, as if she had already decided to keep him. "Yes," the princess told her, making up her mind to adopt the child. In a very smart move, Miriam hurried home and brought Jochebed back to be hired to take care of her own child for the princess. Now that the baby was under the care of Pharaoh's daughter, there was no danger anymore.

The Bible does not tell us how long Moses lived with his own family, but it probably was not more than a few years. Then Jochebed had to give him up again and take him to Pharaoh's palace to be brought up as an Egyptian. But she had trusted God with her son's life and He had cared for him in a miraculous way. God would continue to watch over him. Pharoah's daughter named her adopted son Moses. He lived as a royal son for 40 years.

Baby Moses Action Rhyme

Directions: Teach children this rhyme with the actions. Read the whole story in Exodus 2:1–10.

"Kill all the baby boys!" That's what Pharaoh said.

(*Pound fist into other hand and scowl.*)

What could Moses' family do? Would he soon be dead?

(*Shrug shoulders and hold up hands as if asking a question.*)

Shh, shh, little one. You must not make a sound.

(*Pretend to rock baby in one arm while putting finger of other hand to mouth saying, "Shh."*)

Don't cry! Don't laugh, with soldiers all around!

(*Look fearfully around.*)

Mother makes a basket and places you inside.

(*Pretend to weave a basket.*)

There you go, little one, to take a river ride.

(*Wave goodbye.*)

Rocking gently on the waves, soon you are asleep.

(*Move hands slowly in rocking motion.*)

Without a sound you glide along—not one little peep.

(*Put finger to lips in "shh" motion.*)

Wait a minute! Who is that standing in the water?

(*Point to an imaginary person.*)

Opening up your basket—it looks like Pharaoh's daughter!

(*Bow head and shoulders to royalty.*)

She wants you for her very own; she'll take good care of you.

(*Cross hands over heart.*)

God has had His hand on you because He loves you, too!

(*Point toward heaven; then hold out hand.*)

Baby Trouble in Egypt

Directions: Decode the words to complete the story fact sheet.

A	B	C	D	E	F	G	H	I	J	K	L	M
1	14	2	15	3	16	4	17	5	18	6	19	7

N	O	P	Q	R	S	T	U	V	W	X	Y	Z
20	8	21	9	22	10	23	11	24	12	25	13	26

1. Husband's name: ___ ___ ___ ___ ___
                    1   7   22   1   7

   Wife's name: ___ ___ ___ ___ ___ ___ ___ ___
               18   8   2   17   3   14   3   15

2. What Pharaoh said to do with all Hebrew baby boys: ___ ___ ___ ___ ___ them.
                                                          15   22   8   12   20

3. How long the mother hid her baby boy: ___ ___ ___ ___ ___ months
                                    23   17   22   3   3

4. What the mother hid her baby in: ___ ___ ___ ___ ___ ___
                            14   1   10   6   3   23

5. Who stood guard: ___ ___ ___ ___ ___ ___
                10   5   10   23   3   22

   Her name: ___ ___ ___ ___ ___ ___
           7   5   22   5   1   7

6. Who found the baby: ___ ___ ___ ___ ___ ___ ___ ' ___
                21   17   1   22   1   8   17   10

___ ___ ___ ___ ___ ___ ___ ___
15   1   11   4   17   23   3   22

7. What his adoptive mother named the baby: ___ ___ ___ ___ ___
                                            7   8   10   3   10

Moses Leaves Egypt

(Based on Exodus 2:11–25)

Moses was raised by Pharaoh's daughter as her own son. For 40 years he lived like an Egyptian in the royal family; then one day it all changed. Moses knew that he was Jewish, not Egyptian, by birth, and he felt compassion for his people. He saw how cruelly they were treated by their Egyptian slavemasters, but there was nothing he could do about it. One day he was watching his people as they slaved away at their hard labor. He saw an Egyptian beating one of the Jewish slaves. Moses could not stand it. He looked around and, not seeing anyone else nearby, he went over and grabbed the Egyptian and killed him. Then he quickly dug a hole in the sand and hid the body. The next day Moses saw two Jewish men fighting each other. When he tried to stop the fight, one of the Jews snarled at him, "Who made you ruler and judge over us? Are you thinking of killing me as you killed the Egyptian?"

Suddenly, Moses realized that he must have been seen when he killed the Egyptian. The body must have been discovered! Either that, or the Jewish slave he had rescued had told others about it. Moses had been trying to help his people, but they did not seem to be thankful. Someone would tell Pharaoh what he had done. What should he do? Sure enough, it was not long before Pharaoh found out and gave orders that Moses should be killed. Moses was in big trouble; his Egyptian mother could not keep him out of danger this time, so he ran away. He left Egypt, traveling across the desert to the land of Midian, about 200 miles away. He would be safe from Pharoah's anger there.

Once in Midian, Moses sat down by a well to rest. He watched as seven young women came to the well to get water for their father's sheep. Before they could get any water, some rough shepherds came along and drove them away. Moses came to the girls' rescue and helped them water their sheep. When they got home, the girls told their father, Jethro (also called Reuel), about the Egyptian stranger who had kindly helped them. "Where is he?" their father asked. "Why did you leave him? Invite him to have something to eat." The girls hurried off to find the stranger and invite him home to meet their father.

Jethro, a priest of Midian, invited Moses to stay in his home. Moses agreed, and quickly went from being a well-educated Egyptian prince to being a simple shepherd. He must have wondered why God had allowed such a thing to happen to him.

Moses married Jethro's daughter, Zipporah. They lived in the land of Midian for the next 40 years and had two sons, Gershom and Eliezer. Egypt was the farthest thing from Moses' mind, but God had heard the prayers of the Jewish slaves and He had a plan to deliver them which included Moses!

Out of Egypt Crossword

Directions: Use the clues to complete the crossword puzzle with the correct words. Look up the Bible verses if you need help. **A** words go across; **D** words go down.

CLUES

8-A   Moses killed him for beating a Jewish slave. (Exodus 2:12)

4-A   From whom Moses ran away (Exodus 2:15)

1-D   Where Moses went to live (Exodus 2:15)

5-D   Where Moses sat down to rest (Exodus 2:15)

7-D   How many young women came for water (Exodus 2:16)

7-A   Who drove the women away (Exodus 2:17)

3-D   Who helped the women get water (Exodus 2:17)

6-D   Jethro's (Reuel's) position/title (Exodus 2:16, 18)

2-D   The daughter who married Moses (Exodus 2:21)

Moses' Choice

Directions: Read the Bible verses in the box. Then follow the directions.

> It was by faith that Moses, when he grew up, refused to be called the son of the king of Egypt's daughter. He chose to suffer with God's people instead of enjoying sin for a short time. He thought that it was better to suffer for the Christ than to have all the treasures of Egypt. He was looking only for God's reward.
>
> (Hebrews 11:24–26, New Century Version)

1. Circle the name of the person these verses are about.

2. Draw a light line through what Moses did not want.

3. Draw two lines under what Moses chose instead.

4. Draw a box around the word that tells what Moses had that helped him make this choice.

5. Draw a dashed line under what Moses gave up.

6. Draw three lines under what Moses was looking forward to.

Moses made a wise choice and God blessed him for it. What kinds of choices do you have to make each day?

_____

_____

_____

Read 1 Peter 2:21b to find out how to make wise choices.

The Burning Bush

(Based on Exodus 3)

Moses was taking care of his father-in-law's sheep on the far side of the desert one day when he saw a strange sight. It was a bush that was on fire, but it wasn't burning up! Moses had never seen anything like it before, so he walked closer to get a better look. Suddenly, God spoke to him: "Moses! Moses!"

"Here I am," Moses replied.

God told him not to come any closer to the bush. "Take off your sandals, for the place where you are standing is holy ground," God said. "I am the God of your father, the God of Abraham, the God of Isaac, and the God of Jacob." Moses quickly hid his face because he was afraid to look at God. Why would the great God of Creation be talking to him, a simple shepherd?

God explained to Moses that he had seen the misery of His people in Egypt. He had listened to them cry out to Him and He was concerned about their suffering. "I have come down to rescue them from the hand of the Egyptians," God said, "and to bring them up out of that land into a good and spacious land." And then God said something that made Moses gasp in surprise. "Go," He told Moses. "I am sending you to Pharaoh to bring my people, the Israelites, out of Egypt."

"Surely God could not be planning to use me for such a huge task," thought Moses. "Who am I that I should go to Pharaoh and bring the Israelites out of Egypt?" he asked God.

God did not tell Moses that he was strong or wise or able to do the job better than anyone. God simply said, "I will be with you." That should have been enough to encourage Moses. After all, how could he go wrong when God, Himself, was going with him to help him rescue His people? But Moses wasn't ready to trust God.

"What if I go and the people ask me the name of the One who sent me?" asked Moses.

"Tell them, 'I AM has sent me to you,'" God told him. "Tell them I have watched over them and have seen what has been done to them in Egypt. I will bring them up out of their misery to the land I have promised them." God assured Moses that the Jewish religious leaders would listen to him. They would go with him to Pharaoh to ask him to let all the Jews go into the desert for three days to offer sacrifices to God. Pharaoh would refuse to let them go, so God would strike Egypt with many wonders that would convince Pharaoh. By the time God was through with the Egyptians, they would be pushing the Jews out of the land, even giving them clothes and silver and gold just to get rid of them!

Moses was still afraid to do what the Lord wanted, but he could not change God's plan.

Burning Bush Plaque

Materials

- paper plate
- blue crayon
- dark blue or black marker
- red, yellow, and orange construction paper
- flame patterns (below)
- small evergreen twig
- glue
- sharp pencil
- string
- scissors

Directions

1. Color the paper plate light blue.

2. Using a dark marker, print at the top of the plate: LISTEN! Print at the bottom of the plate: God has something to say to you. (*Optional:* Cut out the word strips below and glue them on the plate instead of printing them.)

3. Glue a small evergreen twig to the center of the plate to look like a bush.

4. Using the two flame patterns above, cut out several red, yellow, and orange flames from construction paper.

5. Arrange the paper flames around, under, and on the twig to look like fire. Glue them into place.

6. Let the glue dry, then poke two small holes in the top of the plate and attach string for a hanger.

7. Talk about how God spoke to Moses through a burning bush. How does God speak to us today?

LISTEN!

God has something to say to you.

Cross Out Message

Directions: What was the first thing God told Moses to do when he came near the burning bush? To find out, cross out the following words in the boxes: Every word that begins with **SH**, every word that ends with **N**, every word that begins with **C**. Write the leftover words on the lines at the bottom of the page.

SHALL	TAKE	CROSS	ON	OFF
CARE	EVEN	YOUR	SANDALS	SHOES
FOR	CALL	THE	PLAN	PLACE
SEEN	WHERE	YOU	SHOULD	CHOOSE
ARE	CANNOT	TURN	STANDING	IN
COULD	SHOW	IS	WIN	SHORT
HOLY	SON	COME	SHUT	GROUND

" _____ _____ _____ _____, _____

_____ _____ _____ _____

_____ _____ _____ _____

_____." (Exodus 3:5)

What God Said

Directions: Circle words in the puzzle to complete the sentences. Look up the Bible verses if you need help. Then write the remaining letters on the lines to find out what God told Moses to say if his people asked him who had sent him.

S	I	E	G	Y	P	T	P
R	A	A	B	M	H	T	H
E	F	N	A	U	R	S	A
S	R	S	D	E	S	E	R
C	A	N	S	A	T	H	A
U	I	E	M	E	L	T	O
E	D	O	Y	O	U	S	H
W	O	N	D	E	R	S	★

1. Moses saw a _____ that was burning, but didn't burn up. (Exodus 3:2)

2. God spoke to Moses from the fire and told him to take off his _____

   because he was standing on holy ground. (Exodus 3:5)

3. Moses hid his face because he was _____. (Exodus 3:6)

4. God had heard the cries of His people in _____. (Exodus 3:7)

5. He was going to _____ them from their slavery. (Exodus 3:8)

6. God was going to send Moses to talk to _____. (Exodus 3:10)

7. Moses would ask that the Jewish people be allowed to go into the

   _____ to offer sacrifices to God. (Exodus 3:18)

8. Though Pharaoh would refuse, God would strike Egypt with _____

   that would make him change his mind. (Exodus 3:20)

   God told Moses, "Tell the people ' ____ ____ ____ ____ ____ ____

   ____ ____ ____ ____ ____ ____ ____ ____ ____ ____ ____ .'" (Exodus 3:14)

Back to Egypt

(Based on Exodus 4:1–6:9)

Though God promised to be with Moses to help him confront his people in Egypt, Moses kept making excuses. "What if the people don't believe me when I say the Lord has sent me?" Moses asked.

God's answer was to point to the staff Moses had in his hand. "Throw it on the ground," He told Moses. When Moses obeyed, the staff turned into a snake and he ran away from it. "Pick it up by the tail," God said. Pick up a poisonous snake by the tail? What could be crazier? But Moses obeyed, and as soon as he touched the snake it turned back into a staff. God told Moses this was a sign he could use to prove that God had sent him to Egypt.

Then God gave him another sign. "Put your hand inside your cloak," He told Moses. After Moses obeyed, he looked at his hand and it was covered with leprosy, a terrible disease for which there was no cure. That must have been a frightening experience for Moses. But the Lord told him to put his diseased hand back inside his cloak again, and when he looked at it, his hand had become restored and well again.

Then God gave Moses a third sign that he could use to prove to his people that God had sent him. "Take some water from the Nile and pour it on the dry ground," God said, "and the water will become blood." Surely Moses' people would believe him when they saw him perform such wonders!

But Moses was still afraid to go to Egypt. He complained that he had never been good at talking to people. "I am slow of speech and tongue," he said.

God knew Moses was just stalling, thinking up excuses for not obeying. "Who gave man his mouth?" God asked. "I will help you speak and will teach you what to say," He promised.

"Please send someone else," Moses begged. God had chosen him for a special job, but Moses didn't have faith to trust God to help him do it. So God said that Moses' brother Aaron could speak for him. Moses would tell him what to say, and Aaron would make the public speeches. Finally, Moses agreed.

Moses told his father-in-law, Jethro, that he was going back to Egypt. He took his wife and two sons and headed across the desert. God reminded Moses that Pharaoh would not do what he asked, but God would convince him. Aaron met Moses on the way and was told exactly what God had said to Moses.

When they arrived in Egypt, the two of them went to talk to the Jewish religious leaders. Aaron told them what God had said to Moses and Moses performed the signs God had given him. The people believed and worshiped God for His plan to save them from slavery and deliver them from Egypt. But Moses and Aaron's first meeting with Pharaoh made the king of Egypt so mad that he immediately made the work even harder for the Jewish slaves. His slave masters were ordered to stop supplying straw to the slaves for making bricks. They had to gather it themselves, but still produce the same number of bricks in a day! Of course, that was impossible, and the Jews were beaten even worse than before. They complained to Moses that he had not helped them, but had just made their lives more miserable.

Moses prayed and the Lord told him to tell the people, "I will take you as my own people, and I will be your God. I will free you from your slavery." But the Jewish slaves were too discouraged to listen.

What Happened Next?

Directions: Draw what happened when Moses did what God said. Look up the Bible verses if you need help.

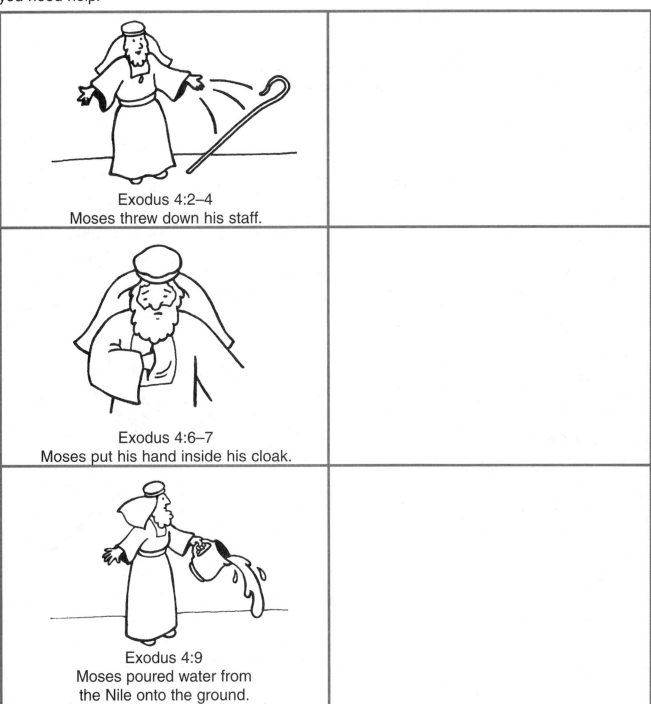

Exodus 4:2–4
Moses threw down his staff.

Exodus 4:6–7
Moses put his hand inside his cloak.

Exodus 4:9
Moses poured water from the Nile onto the ground.

Why did God have Moses perform these signs?

_____

When Trouble Comes

The Jewish leaders praised God when Moses told them He was going to deliver His people. But how did the Jewish slaves respond when their troubles got worse instead of better? They got angry at Moses and were too discouraged to even listen when God reminded them of His care.

How does God want us to respond when trouble comes? To find out, solve the clues. Then use the words to complete the Bible verse. Look up Psalm 59:16 to check your work.

Clues

1. Power <u>s</u> __ __ __ __ __ __

2. Make music with your voice __ __ __ __

3. Opposite of "you" __

4. Opposite of "evening" __ __ __ __ __ __ __

5. Stronghold <u>f</u> __ __ __ __ __ __

6. Hard times; difficulty <u>t</u> __ __ __ __ __ __

7. Opposite of "my" __ __ __ __

8. Opposite of "out" __ __

9. Opposite of "hate" __ __ __ __

10. A place of safety <u>r</u> __ __ __ __ __ __

11. Replace the "d" in "dimes" with a "t" __ __ __ __ __

12. Replace the 'd' in "bud" to a "t" __ __ __

13. Opposite of "won't" __ __ __ __

14. Opposite of "me" __ __ __

15. Replace the "g" in "age" with an "r" __ __ __

16. Opposite of #7 __ __

_____ _____ _____ _____ of _____

_____, _____ the _____ _____ _____

_____ of _____ _____; for _____

_____ _____, _____

_____ _____ of _____.

The Ten Plagues

(Based on Exodus 7–12)

Moses did as God had [told] him and asked Pharaoh to let the Jews (now called Israelites) leave Egypt for three days to [go] into the desert and offer sacrifices to God. Pharaoh refused, just as God had said he would. No[w] God began a series of plagues on Egypt to change Pharaoh's mind and to demonstrate God's pow[er] to the Egyptians.

The first plague was o[n the] Nile River. Moses told Pharaoh that since he had not listened to the Lord's request to let H[is p]eople go, the water of the river would turn to blood. Moses struck the water with his staff an[d it] turned to blood. All the fish died and the Egyptians were not able to drink the water. In fact, eve[n th]e water in ponds and canals and in people's water jars turned to blood! But Pharaoh refused.

A week later, Moses [spo]ke with Pharaoh again. When he still wouldn't listen, God sent a plague of frogs on Egypt. T[hey] were everywhere—in the palace, in people's ovens, covering the ground. Then Pharaoh told M[ose]s he would let the Jews go if he would just get rid of the frogs. However, when Moses did wh[at h]e asked, Pharaoh broke his promise and refused to let the people go.

When Pharaoh refus[ed] Moses' third request, God turned the dust into gnats. They covered Egypt, biting and crawling [on] people and animals. It was terrible, but Pharaoh would not give in.

A fourth time, Mos[es a]sked for Pharaoh's permission to take his people into the desert. When the king once more refu[sed], God sent swarms of flies over the land. Pharaoh said he'd let the people go if Moses got rid of [the] flies, but when the flies were gone, Pharaoh changed his mind again.

The fifth time Mos[es a]sked Pharaoh to let his people go, God struck the livestock with a plague. Most of the Egypti[ans'] animals died, but all the animals belonging to the Israelites were fine. Still Pharaoh refused to [let] the people go.

Then God told Mo[ses] and Aaron to take handfuls of soot from a furnace and toss it into the air. When they did, pa[inf]ul sores broke out upon the bodies of the Egyptians and the animals that were left. In spite of h[is p]eople's suffering from the sixth plague, Pharaoh stubbornly refused to give in.

Moses warned Ph[ara]oh that if he didn't let the Israelites go, God would send the worst hailstorm Egypt had ever se[en.] The Egyptians were warned to put their animals in shelters and stay inside, themselves. Som[e d]id what Moses said. When the hail came they were safe, but those who had not listened were kil[led] by the hail. Pharaoh told Moses to stop the hail and he would give in, then he changed his min[d.]

When Pharaoh r[efu]sed Moses' request again, God sent the eighth plague, locusts to devour every plant in the land[. P]haraoh's officials advised him to let the people go, but Pharaoh would not listen.

Then God sent [ful]l darkness over the land for three days. Only the Israelites had light. Pharaoh almost gave in, [the]n changed his mind again. He angrily told Moses he never wanted to see him again.

The tenth plag[ue w]as the worst. Moses warned Pharaoh that God would take the life of the oldest son in every E[gy]ptian family. Pharaoh did not give in until his own son was one of those killed. Finally, he agr[eed] that Moses could take his people into the desert. The Egyptian people wanted the Israelites o[ut] of their land so God would quit punishing them. They gave God's people gold and silver and clo[th]ing as parting gifts. And so God's people left, not just for a three-day trip to the desert, but fo[r a] long journey to the land God had promised them.

Plague Puzzle

Directions: Match each of the ten pictures with the plagues by writing the correct letter on each one. Then write a number between 1 and 10 on it to show the order of it.

A. Locusts

B. Darkness

C. River Turned to Blood

D. Frogs

E. Flies

F. Gnats

G. Death of Oldest Sons

H. Boils

I. Death of Livestock

J. Hail

Mighty Deeds Booklet

Students will enjoy making this booklet as a reminder of God's power in Moses' day and today.

Materials

- 8 ½" x 11" sheet of paper
- plague pictures on this page
- scissors
- glue
- fine-tip dark marker
- paper clip
- tape

Directions

1. Cut the sheet of paper in half lengthwise.

2. Tape the two long pieces of paper end-to-end to make a long strip.

3. Divide the paper strip into sections slightly less than 2 $\frac{1}{4}$" long and fold it accordion style.

4. Cut out the plague pictures on this page and glue them in order on the accordion folded pages.

5. Write on each page a description of the plague.

6. Print this Bible verse on the back of the folded pages, one or two words on each page: "I will remember the deeds of the LORD; yes, I will remember your miracles of long ago." (Psalm 77:11)

7. Use a paper clip to hold the pages flat when you're not reading it.

Our Mighty God

Directions: Read Psalm 105:26–38 to see how the psalm writer described our mighty God's plagues on Egypt. Then use the clues to complete the acrostic.

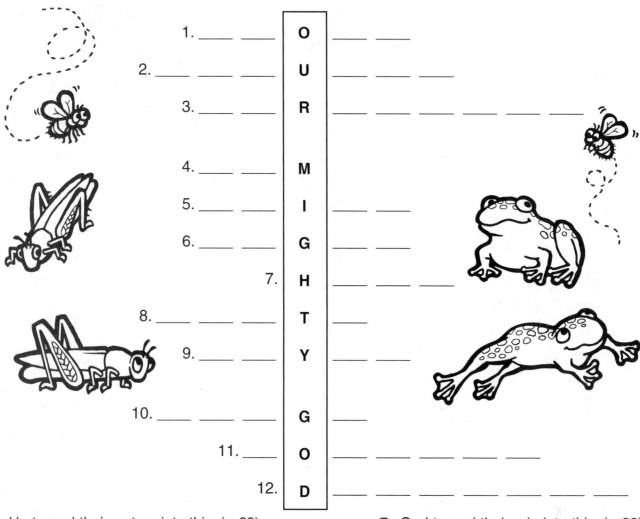

1. ___ ___ **O** ___ ___

2. ___ ___ ___ **U** ___ ___ ___

3. ___ ___ ___ **R** ___ ___ ___ ___ ___ ___

4. ___ ___ **M**

5. ___ ___ **I** ___

6. ___ ___ **G** ___

7. **H** ___ ___ ___

8. ___ ___ ___ **T** ___

9. ___ ___ ___ **Y** ___

10. ___ ___ **G** ___

11. ___ **O** ___ ___ ___ ___

12. **D** ___ ___ ___ ___ ___ ___ ___

1. He turned their waters into this. (v. 29)

2. God spoke, and these came. (v. 34)

3. He struck down all these. (v. 36)

4. Another name for Egypt, the Land of ___ (v. 27)

5. He spoke, and swarms of these bugs came. (v. 31)

6. Moses and Aaron performed these. (v. 27)

7. God turned their rain into this. (v. 32)

8. More bugs, tiny ones! (v. 31)

9. ___ was glad when they left. (v. 38)

10. Their land teemed with these. (v. 30)

11. Another word for miracles (v. 27)

12. God sent this on the land. (v. 28)

What two plagues didn't the psalm writer mention? _____

and _____

The First Passover

(Based on Exodus 12)

Before God sent the tenth plague on the land of Egypt, he told Moses to warn the Jewish people. "About midnight I will go throughout Egypt," God told him. "Every firstborn son in Egypt will die, from the firstborn son of Pharaoh, who sits on the throne, to the firstborn son of the slave girl, who is at her hand mill, and all the firstborn of the cattle as well." Then he explained to Moses exactly what his people needed to do.

Each family was to take a lamb and care for it for two weeks. At the end of that time, the father of the family should kill the lamb, then smear some of its blood on the sides and top of their door. That night the family was to roast the lamb and eat all of it with bitter herbs and flat bread (made without yeast). The people were to eat the meal quickly, dressed for traveling, ready to leave at any moment. They must stay inside and not go out of their houses for any reason. That night the Lord would strike down the firstborn male, men and animals, in every household. However, he would pass over every home that had blood on the top and sides of the door. "When I see the blood, I will pass over you," He promised. "No destructive plague will touch you when I strike Egypt."

That day was to be a special day of celebration, called Passover, every year after that for the Jewish people. In the future, the celebration would begin with eating flat bread for seven days and doing no work except to prepare food. All yeast would be taken out of every Jewish house. Then on the day of Passover, the family would eat the same meal that was eaten at the first Passover: roast lamb with bitter herbs and flat bread.

The bread without yeast was a reminder of how the people had to be ready to leave at a moment's notice, as soon as Pharaoh told Moses they could go. The roast lamb reminded them of the lamb that was killed so they wouldn't have to be. It was the lamb's blood that protected them. The bitter herbs were a reminder of the trouble and bitter experiences the Jews had faced in Eygpt.

The first Passover was a frightening experience for Egyptians and Israelites alike. As God's people waited through the night behind closed doors, listening to the weeping and wailing of Egyptians whose family members had suddenly died, they must have wondered if Pharaoh would finally let them go. Then in the middle of the night word came that it was time to leave. Four centuries of Jewish slavery in Eygpt was over at last! The people grabbed their few possessions which were packed and ready and, urged on by their Egyptian neighbors with gifts of gold and silver and clothes, they walked away, more than two million of them!

Passover is a celebration still observed every year by Jewish people, a joyful occasion to remember how God rescued His people.

Passover Song

Directions: Sing this song with your students. Challenge them to come up with appropriate actions to do as they sing it.

(*Tune:* "I Will Make You Fishers of Men")

God said, "Take the blood of a lamb, blood of a lamb, blood of a lamb."

God said, "Take the blood of a lamb; put it on your door.

Put it on your door; put it on your door."

God said, "Take the blood of a lamb; put it on your door."

"That night I will pass over you, pass over you, pass over you.

That night I will pass over you and you will be saved.

And you will be saved; yes you will be saved.

That night I will pass over you and you will be saved."

Jesus is my Passover lamb, Passover lamb, Passover lamb;

Jesus is my Passover lamb, for He died for me.

Jesus died for me; yes, He died for me.

Jesus is my Passover lamb, for He died for me.

Discussion

At the first Passover, what would have happened to anyone who did not believe in God or trust the lamb's blood to keep them safe? How is Jesus your Passover lamb? Is He everyone's Passover lamb? Why or why not?

Passover Dot-to-Dot

Directions: Connect the numbered dots to complete something that is a very important part of Passover.

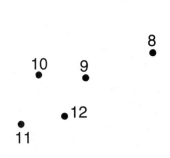
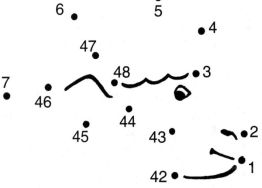

6
5
47
4
8
48
3
7
10   9
46
12
45   44
11
43   2
42   1

41

40
13
14   21   28   30   34   35   39
15   20   29
22   27
25   37
18   26   32
16   23   24   36   38
17   19   31   33

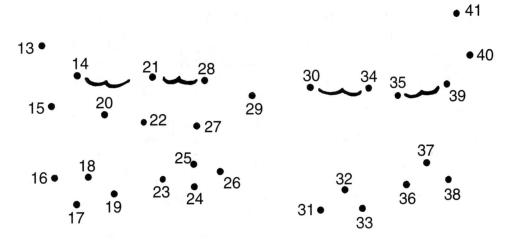

Why is this thing such an important part of Passover?

_____

_____

Directions: Draw what is missing on the picture.

Crossing the Red Sea

(Based on Exodus 13:17–15:21)

Finally, God's people were on their way out of Egypt. God led them across the desert toward the Red Sea. He went ahead of them in a tall cloud by day and at night the cloud became fire which gave them light so they could continue traveling in the dark. God warned Moses that Pharaoh would come after them, but He would protect His people.

Sure enough, when Pharaoh heard that the Israelites had left the country rather than just going for a three-day trip into the desert, he became angry. He was suddenly upset that he had lost their services as slaves, so he decided to go after them and bring them back. He got in his chariot and led his whole army with more than 600 chariots after the Israelites. Long before the Egyptians reached them, the Israelites could see their dust in the distance. They immediately accused Moses of putting them in danger. "Didn't we tell you to leave us alone?" they said. "Why didn't you just let us serve the Egyptians? It would have been better than dying in the desert!" Already, Moses' people had forgotten how they had suffered in slavery.

"Don't be afraid," Moses told them. "Stand firm and you will see the deliverance the LORD will bring you today. The LORD will fight for you; you need only to be still."

"Tell the Israelties to move on," God said to Moses. Then He told Moses to hold up his staff toward the sea. When Moses obeyed, a strong wind came and began to drive the sea back. The waters divided and a dry path appeared across the sea with a wall of water on each side. The Israelites began hurrying across the sea before the Egyptians could catch up with them. As they walked across the sea, God moved the cloud of His Presence behind them, coming between them and the Egyptian army. The cloud brought light to the Israelites and darkness to the Egyptians all night long.

When the Egyptians finally saw what was happening, they drove their chariots down to the sea and began chasing the Israelites. God made their chariot wheels come off to slow them down. Some of the Egyptians recognized that their trouble came from God. They said, "Let's get away from the Israelites!" But before they could go back, God told Moses to stretch his hand out toward the sea again. When he did, the water suddenly began flowing again and the dry path disappeared. The sea went back to its place and all the Egyptian soldiers who had followed the Israelites across the sea were drowned.

All the Israelites made it safely across the sea to the other side. "When the Israelites saw the great power the LORD displayed against the Egyptians, the people feared the LORD and put their trust in him." Moses and the Israelites sang a song of praise to God while his sister Miriam and all the women danced and sang with tambourines.

Once again the Lord had saved His people with a miracle!

Red Sea Maze

Directions: Help the Israelites find their way across the desert to the Red Sea to go across on dry ground.

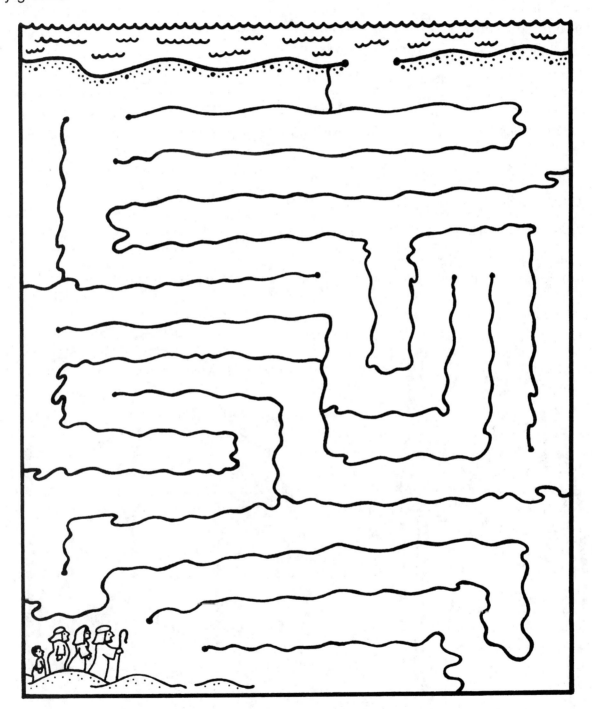

Why did God save His people again? Read Psalm 106:7–9 to find out.

Parting the Sea Picture

Have students make this fold-up picture to illustrate the story of God's people at the Red Sea. You will find the whole story in Exodus 14:5–31.

1. Copy the scene on page 29 and the figures of Moses and the Israelites below.

2. Color the scene and color and cut out the two figures.

3. Fold the scene on the dashed lines so the path across the sea is completely hidden.

4. Lightly tape the figures of Moses on the right fold and the Israelites on the left fold.

5. Use a blue marker or crayon to draw waves above the figures to represent the waters of the Red Sea.

6. With the scene folded, it shows what happened in the Bible story when God's people got to the Red Sea. Moses raised his staff toward the sea as God told him and the people watched. When the scene is unfolded, the dry path God made across the sea appears. Carefully take the figures of Moses and the Israelites off the folded back of the scene and tape them to the path across the sea.

7. Finally, refold the scene and remove Moses and the Israelites, taping them back on the folds again to show how Moses raised his staff again and the waters of the sea closed back up.

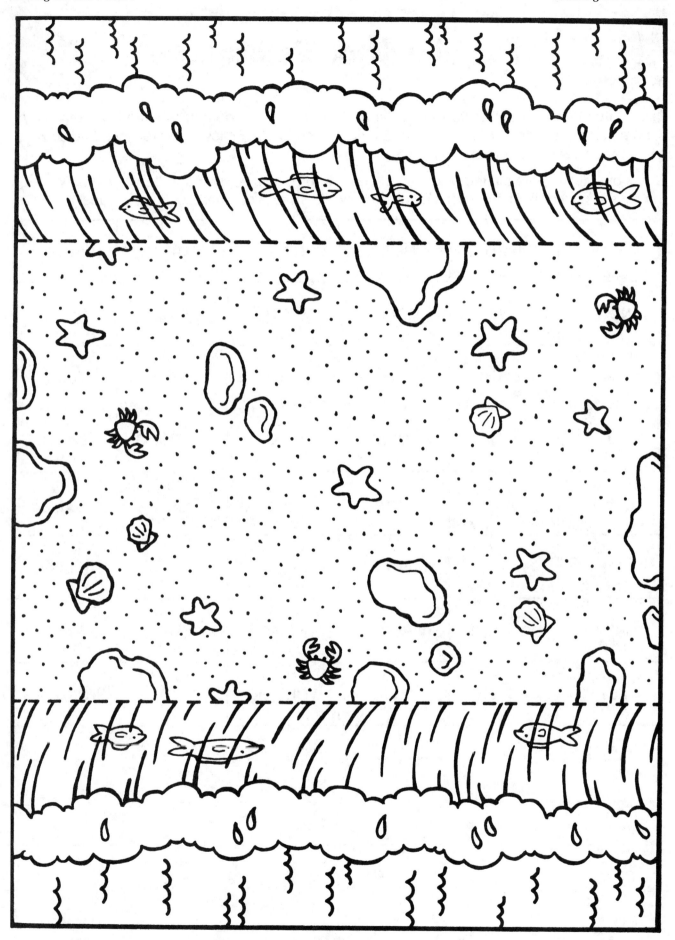

Words of Praise

Directions: When the Israelites saw what the Lord did to get them across the Red Sea, they sang a song of praise to Him. You can read it in Exodus 15. Follow the directions to discover some of their words of praise.

Cross out all the words in the boxes that: begin with **n**, rhyme with **cast**, begin with **s**. Write the remaining words in order on the lines below. To check your work look up Exodus 15:11.

LAST	WHO	NEW	SELF	AMONG	SHOULD
NOW	THE	GODS	NATION	SIGN	NIGHT
IS	LIKE	SO	NONE	YOU	SAVE
O	NOT	LORD	WHO	NOTHING	SHALL
NEAR	IS	SOME	LIKE	FAST	SAME
YOU	SINCE	MAJESTIC	SOON	IN	BLAST
SHINE	HOLINESS	AWESOME	NAME	IN	PAST
GLORY	NEVER	SEEM	WORKING	NO	WONDERS

_____ _____ _____ _____ _____ _____

_____, _____ _____? _____ _____

_____ — _____ _____ _____,

_____ _____ _____,

_____ _____? (Exodus 15:11)

In the Desert

(Based on Exodus 15:22–17:16)

The Israelites were across the Red Sea and most of Pharaoh's army had been drowned chasing them. Now they didn't have to worry about the Egyptians anymore. They didn't have to keep looking over their shoulders to see if they were being followed. They could relax and trust God. They traveled in the desert for three days without finding any water. Then, when they finally found water it was too bitter to drink. The people grumbled and complained. Moses prayed. The Lord had Moses throw a piece of wood into the water and the bitterness went away. The people drank thirstily until they were satisfied. Then God said to His people, "If you listen carefully to the voice of the LORD your God and do what is right in his eyes, if you pay attention to his commands and keep all his decrees, I will not bring on you any of the diseases I brought on the Egyptians, for I am the LORD, who heals you." Would the people listen and obey?

Their next stop was Elim where there were 12 springs of water and 70 palm trees, a real oasis in the desert. They camped there, enjoying the security of having water so near. But they had many miles to go, so they left and headed for the Desert of Sin. While they were in the desert the people began complaining again. They fondly remembered the good food they had eaten in Egypt, forgetting all the pain and suffering they had also experienced there. "We ate all the food we wanted," they said to Moses, "but you have brought us out into this desert to starve this entire assembly to death." God was faithful in spite of His people's unfaithfulness. He promised to send them bread from heaven, but he made certain rules about gathering the bread. Each day they were to gather only enough food for that day. But on the sixth day they were permitted to gather twice as much so they wouldn't have to go out and gather on the Sabbath. This was God's way of testing His people's obedience. Then God said to Moses, "I have heard the grumbling of the Israelites. Tell them that at twilight they will eat meat and in the morning they will be filled with bread. Then they will know that I am the Lord their God." That evening, quail came and covered the camp. The people killed the birds and ate the tasty meat. The next morning when the dew on the ground was gone, in its place were thin, white flakes. It was God's bread for the people. They gathered it and ate it. It was sweet like wafers made with honey. The people called it manna (which means "what is it?"). Of course, some of the people disobeyed God's instructions and tried to pick up enough manna to last them several days! But when they got up the next morning, they found that all the extra manna they had gathered had spoiled and couldn't be eaten. For the 40 years that God's people wandered in the desert on the way to the Promised Land, He provided manna every morning for them. God told Moses to gather a container of manna and keep it for future generations to show what God had done for His people. The manna Moses gathered and saved did not spoil. Later Moses placed it in the Ark of the Covenant.

Sometime later, the people stopped at Rephidim. Again they were thirsty and there was no water, so they complained to Moses and accused him of bringing them into the desert to die. God told Moses to strike a rock with his staff and water gushed out, enough for everyone.

While they were at Rephidim, Amalekites attacked the Israelites. Joshua led the Israelites as they fought an all-day battle. Moses stood on a hill with his hands raised and God helped the Israelites win. Every time Moses lowered his hands to rest, the Amalekites began winning. Finally Aaron and Hur had Moses sit down and they held his hands up until the battle was over. God gave the Israelites victory over the Amalekites that day.

"God Provides" Poem

Directions: Read the poem. Fill in the missing words. Make sure each one rhymes with the other line.

God Provides

(Based on Psalm 78:11–29)

God's people forgot what he had done for them in Egypt land;

The wonders that He had performed, the rescue He had _____.

When Pharaoh's army came for them, God opened up the sea.

The people crossed upon dry ground, no longer slaves but _____!

God led them in a cloud by day and showed them where to _____.

By night He warmed them with His fire; God loved His people so.

He split a rock and water flowed when they complained of _____.

Did they thank Him? Not at all! And that was not the worst.

Soon they got hungry and complained they were about to _____!

With fondness they recalled the food in Egypt with a sigh.

"Will you let us starve to death?" they screamed at Moses then.

And raining meat and bread on them, God blessed them once _____.

They ate the bread of heaven and gobbled down the _____,

But did not stop to thank the Lord for giving food to eat.

Manna from Heaven Skit

Characters: Adult Israelites—Joab, Hannah, and Moses; Israelite Children—Joel, Bitsy, Rebekah, and David

Props: small bits of paper scattered on the floor; baskets

Moses: (*Speaking to all the characters above*) Friends, listen to me! You have complained of hunger, so God has promised to give us special bread to eat. Tomorrow morning it will be here for you to gather. But you must only gather enough for the day for your family—no more! On the day before the Sabbath you may gather extra because God will not provide it on the Sabbath.

Joab: (*Talking to Hannah*) It's about time God gave us some decent food! The quail was good, but who wants to eat quail all the time?

Hannah: Well, I don't know. God seems to be providing for us. I hate to complain.

Joab: Well, I don't! I miss the wonderful food we had in Egypt. Sometimes I wish we were back there.

Hannah: Oh no! That would be terrible! Don't you remember how we were mistreated? It was a horrible life!

Joab: Well, at least we we didn't go hungry and we had plenty of water to drink. This desert trip is turning out to be a real pain! And I don't think much of Moses as a leader.

Bitsy: (*Walking up to Joab*) Uncle Joab, Aunt Rachel says she needs you.

Joab: All right! Good night, Hannah. (*Walking off with Bitsy.*)

Hannah: (*Looking toward heaven*) Lord God, I'm afraid some of us are not very grateful for the way You have been providing for us. As I stand here in the dark and see your pillar of fire, I know You are with us. Thank You for bringing us out of Egypt and for leading us on this journey. (*Walks away*)

Joel: (*Yawning and stretching, then looking at the ground*) Hey, what's that stuff? It looks like frost, but it isn't cold enough for that. (*Touches the floor with one finger, then puts finger in mouth*) Wow! That's good! Hey David, Rebekah, come here, quick!

David: (*Running out*) What are you yelling about? What's going on?

Rebekah: (*Walking out with Bitsy*) What's all the fuss about, Joel?

Bitsy: Yah, did you see an angel or something?

Joel: Look around you, on the ground. (*They all look at the floor*)

Bitsy: What is it?

Joel: It's food, that's what! Go ahead, taste it. (*Touches the floor with finger and puts finger in mouth*)

David: (*Touches the floor with finger and puts finger in mouth*) Hey! That's good! Kind of sweet.

Rebekah: (*Touches the floor with finger and puts finger in mouth*) Yummy! This must be the bread from heaven Moses said God would send us. I'm going to get my basket! (*runs off*)

Bitsy: Mama! Mama! There's food on the ground! (*runs off*)

(*Joel and David keep putting their fingers on the floor, then in their mouths. Rebekah comes back with baskets.*)

Rebekah: Here, you are. Quit snacking and start gathering so your families can have some breakfast. (*Rebekah, Joel, and David begin picking up bits of paper and putting them in the baskets*)

Bitsy: See! I told you so! Looky, looky! (*runs in with a basket, pulling Hannah by the hand*)

Hannah: (*Bending down to pick up a bit of paper*) Why, it is food. (*puts her finger in her mouth*) And so tasty. How amazing!

Manna from Heaven Skit

Bitsy: Can I gather the, "what is it," Mama? Please?

Hannah: Of course, dear. You start while I go tell the others about this. *(walks off)*

David: Have you ever seen anything like this? *(holding up a bit of paper and inspecting it)* And it doesn't taste like anything I've ever tasted before. *(putting his finger in his mouth)*

Rebekah: David! Quit eating and keep gathering or there'll be none left for your family.

Joel: I guess this is kind of a miracle, isn't it? I mean, there's no way this could have just happened.

Bitsy: Of course it's a miracle. And this isn't the first one God has done for us. Remember all the wonders He did in Egypt?

David: Yes, but those were scary miracles. This is a really nice one.

Joel: When Moses hit the rock and water came out for us to drink, do you think that was a miracle?

David: Sure! Moses could have spent the whole day hitting desert rocks and not found any water.

Rebekah: Yes, God definitely provided that water.

David: And when Moses threw that stick into the water at Marah and the water lost its bitterness, that was a miracle. Wasn't it?

Joel: I guess so. Sometimes God's miracles just look like regular stuff, so I forget that it might be God working.

Bitsy: God is working all the time; that's what Mama says. He leads us every day by the cloud that goes in front of us and He's with us every night in the pillar of fire.

Hannah: *(walking in with Joab, pointing at the floor)* Now be careful where you step because it's everywhere. You don't want to ruin it.

Joab: Are you sure it's safe for the children to be eating this? It might be poisonous.

Hannah: Oh, Joab, this is God's food for us. Of course it's safe. *(begins gathering "manna")*

Bitsy: *(standing up and gesturing)* Come on, everybody! There's enough for all of us. Bread—special delivery from God!

Joab: Well, I don't know about this.

David: Taste it, father. Go ahead, it's good.

Joab: *(Touches the floor with finger and puts finger in mouth; then smiles)* My, that is good! Let's load up more baskets, David.

Rebekah: Sir? Moses said we were only to gather enough for today.

Joab: Now, now, little girl, I know what I'm doing. If we get a lot of it today, then we won't have to come out and gather it again for two or three days. *(begins gathering paper bits and putting them in a basket)*

(Everyone leaves. Joel comes back in giggling; then Rebekah and Bitsy come in.)

Rebekah: What's so funny, Joel?

Joel: *(laughing)* Remember how David and his dad gathered four baskets of God's bread yesterday so they wouldn't have to come out and get more today?

Rebekah: Yes. So?

Joel: So, go smell their tent! All the extra bread spoiled and their tent smells so bad they had to move in with David's uncle. *(laughs more)*

Bitsy: Well, Uncle Joab should have known better. Moses warned us. Some people just don't listen. Let's get some more "what is it."

Rebekah: Let's call it "manna." That means "what is it." We may not know what it is, but we know where it's from—bread from heaven, sent to us by God!

Water from the Rock

Directions: Cut out the picture on this page and color it. Then fold back the right third of the picture on the dashed lines. Tell the story of the people's thirst and how God told Moses to strike a rock with his staff to get water. Then unfold the picture to show water gushing from the rock just as God promised.

Moses struck the rock and water flowed!

Exodus 17:1–6

The Ten Commandments

(Based on Exodus 19–20; 32)

Three months after the Israeltes left Egypt they came to Mount Sinai. They camped, and Moses went up the mountain to talk to God. The Lord said the people should get ready because He was going to come down the mountain in a cloud so they could see Him. Three days later a thick cloud came over the mountain with thunder and lightning. The people heard a loud trumpet blast and they trembled with fear. Moses led them to the foot of the mountain. Suddenly, the mountain was covered with smoke and the whole mountain shook. The trumpet got louder and louder. Moses spoke to God and God answered. Then Moses and Aaron went up the mountain where the Lord gave Moses His Ten Commandments.

God said:

"You shall have no other gods before me.

You shall not make for yourself an idol. You shall not bow down to them or worship them.

You shall not misuse the name of the LORD your God

Remember the Sabbath day by keeping it holy.

Honor your father and your mother.

You shall not murder.

You shall not commit adultery.

You shall not steal.

You shall not give false testimony against your neighbor.

You shall not covet anything that belongs to your neighbor."

When the people saw thunder, lightning, and smoke on the mountain and heard the trumpet, they were frightened. They told Moses they did not want to have God speak to them. They wanted Moses to tell them what God said. Moses tried to convince them that they had no reason to be afraid, but the people stayed at a distance as Moses went back up the mountain to talk with God.

God gave Moses more rules for His people to obey, rules about servants, personal injury, property, festivals, and instructions for building the tabernacle. Moses was gone a long time and some of the people became restless. They asked Aaron to make them an idol. Amazingly, Aaron agreed to help the people make an idol they could worship in place of the one true God! The people gave him their gold jewelry. He melted the gold in a fire; then he shaped it into an idol that looked like a calf. Aaron built an altar in front of the golden calf idol and the people offered burnt sacrifices to it and celebrated their new idol.

God knew what was happening, so He sent Moses back down the mountain. When Moses saw the people dancing and bowing down to the calf idol he was so angry he threw down the stone tablets which contained the Ten Commandments and they broke. Aaron said he had taken the people's gold jewelry and thrown it into the fire and the calf had come out! Moses crushed the idol into tiny pieces, then ground it up, put it in water and made the people drink it. About 3,000 of the people died that day because of their sin. The people who had not sinned continued with Moses toward the Promised Land.

Seeing God

Directions: God told Moses He was going to show Himself to the people and speak to them. But the way God appeared to the people scared them so much they wouldn't even come near! Find and circle in the word search puzzle seven things the people saw and heard. Then write the remaining letters in order on the lines to find out what the people said to Moses. The lines on the left are clues to help you figure out what words are hidden in the puzzle. You can read the story in Exodus 19:16–19; 20:18–21.

T _ _ _ _ _ _ _ _

L _ _ _ _ _ _ _ _ _

C _ _ _ _ _

F _ _ _ _

S _ _ _ _

T _ _ _ _ _ _ _

B _ _ _ _

THE MOUNTAIN

T _ _ _ _ _ _ _ _

VIOLENTLY

T	R	E	M	B	L	E	D
B	H	U	T	D	O	N	L
T	R	U	M	P	E	T	I
O	T	H	N	K	A	V	G
E	G	O	O	D	D	F	H
S	P	M	U	E	E	I	T
A	S	O	K	T	O	R	N
B	L	A	S	T	U	E	I
C	S	O	R	W	E	W	N
I	L	L	D	I	E	✡	G

THE PEOPLE SAID TO MOSES, "SPEAK TO US YOURSELF AND WE WILL LISTEN.

_ _ _ _ _ _ _ _ _ _ _ _ _

_ _ _ _ _ _ _ _ _ _ _ _ _

_ _ _ _ _ _ _ _ _ _ ."

Commandment Code

The Ten Commandments

Directions: Decode the Ten Commandments. Then number them to put them in correct order. Check your work by looking up Exodus 20:1–17.

CODE

A	B	C	D	E	F	G	H	I	J	K	L	M
✡	✳	♣	●	■	❑	◗	❄	†	▼	✎	✗	✔

N	O	P	Q	R	S	T	U	V	W	X	Y	Z
◼	✺	⊕	○	↔	{	➢	↕	❘	☞	☎	✈	✂

____ You shall have no other ____ ____ ____ ____ before me.
(◗ ✺ ● {)

____ You shall not commit ____ ____ ____ ____ ____ ____ ____ ____.
(✡ ● ↕ ✗ ➢ ■ ↔ ✈)

____ You shall not make an ____ ____ ____ ____ to worship.
(† ● ✺ ✗)

____ You shall not ____ ____ ____ ____ ____ ____.
(✔ ↕ ↔ ● ■ ↔)

____ You shall not misuse the ____ ____ ____ ____ of the LORD your God.
(◼ ✡ ✔ ■)

____ Remember the Sabbath day by keeping it ____ ____ ____ ____.
(❄ ✺ ✗ ✈)

____ You shall not give ____ ____ ____ ____ ____ testimony against your neighbor.
(❑ ✡ ✗ { ■)

____ You shall not ____ ____ ____ ____ ____.
({ ➢ ■ ✡ ✗)

____ Honor your ____ ____ ____ ____ ____ ____ and your ____ ____ ____ ____ ____ ____.
(❑ ✡ ➢ ❄ ■ ↔)   (✔ ✺ ➢ ❄ ■ ↔)

____ You shall not ____ ____ ____ ____ ____ anything that belongs to your neighbor.
(♣ ✺ ❘ ■ ➢)

The Purpose of the Law

Directions: What was the purpose of God's Law, the Ten Commandments? To find out, write on the lines below every other letter in the chart. When you get to the end of a line, continue to the next line, following the arrows. Look up Galatians 3:24 to check your work.

B	T	E	H	F	E	O	L	R	A	E	W	T	W
N	T	I	I	T	A	U	F	P	S	S	I	A	H
H	C	C	H	A	A	M	R	E	G	W	E	E	T
S	L	U	E	D	H	A	E	R	L	E	O	W	
O	T	P	O	R	C	I	H	S	R	O	I	N	S
E	H	W	T	T	Y	A	B	H	S	T	R	T	E
E	M	L	I	A	G	W	H	L	T	O	B	C	E
I	N	F	U	I	P	T	U	S	D	U	E	J	K
L	E	E	D	P	B	U	Y	N	F	T	A	I	I
†	†	†	†	†	†	†	†			A	H	F	T	I

___ ___ ___ ___ ___ ___ ___ ___

___ ___ ___ ___ ___ ___ ___ ___ ___ ___ ___

___ ___ ___ ___ ___ ___ ___ ___ ___

___ ___ ___ ___ ___ ___ ___ ___ ___

___ ___ ___ ___ ___. (Galatians 3:24)

Building the Tabernacle

(Based on Exodus 35–40)

God gave Moses instructions for building a sanctuary for Him and He promised to dwell among them there. "Make this tabernacle and all its furnishings exactly like the pattern I will show you," God told him. Moses listened carefully, then explained God's plan to His people. The plans began with an offering to the Lord from each person. These were not like the usual offerings, but were special materials that would be used for the tabernacle: gold, silver, and bronze; blue, purple, and scarlet yarn; fine linen; goat hair; ram skins dyed red and hides of sea cows; acacia wood; olive oil; spices; onyx stones and other gems.

The people willingly gave their offerings to the project. In fact, Moses had to send out word that they had more than enough materials for the tabernacle, so people should stop giving! The Lord told Moses to appoint a man named Bezalel to be in charge of artistic design. He taught other workers how to cut and set stones, to work in wood, and to do artistic designs with gold, silver, and bronze. Other artistic people wove and embroidered with yarn and fine linen. Some men who were skilled in woodwork built frames of acacia wood. The frames were then covered with animal skins. Everything was done exactly as the Lord told Moses so the tabernacle could be set up, then taken down and packed to carry along from place to place as the Israelites traveled to the Promised Land.

Only the finest materials were used for such an important project. The tabernacle was about 45 feet long and 15 feet wide and high. The ark of the covenant was a box built of acacia wood, a hard wood that would last for years. It was about 3¼ feet long and 2½ feet wide and high and covered with pure gold, inside and out. The cover was made of gold with two golden angels (cherubim) facing each other with their wings spread over the ark.

Inside the tabernacle, the space was separated into The Most Holy Place (Holy of Holies) where the ark was kept and The Holy Place, the area outside The Most Holy Place. Outside the tent was a large courtyard where the altar for burnt offerings was located. Near the altar was a large basin which was to be kept filled with water so the priests could wash themselves before offering burnt sacrifices to the Lord. The Most Holy Place was closed off by a beautiful curtain. Only the High Priest was allowed inside once a year on the Day of Atonement.

When all the work was finished, Moses had everything put in place; then God's cloud of glory filled the tabernacle. God was pleased with the work Moses and His people had done. As long as the cloud stayed in the tabernacle, the Israelites stayed where they were, but when the glory cloud lifted above the tabernacle, the people knew God was directing them to continue their journey toward the Promised Land. Then they would carefully disassemble the tabernacle, pack it, and carry it to the next stop on their travels.

A long time later, after the Israelites had lived in the Promised Land for many years, God chose King Solomon to build a temple for Him. Since His people were no longer traveling but had settled down in the land, they needed a permanent place to worship. The great temple Solomon built was much grander than the tabernacle had been, but the basic plan was the same with The Most Holy Place, The Holy Place, and the Courtyard.

What's in the Ark?

Directions: What was kept inside the Ark of the Covenant? Draw a line from the ark to each of the three items below that you think were in the ark. Look up Hebrews 9:3–4 to see if you are right. Why do you think God chose these items to be put inside the ark?

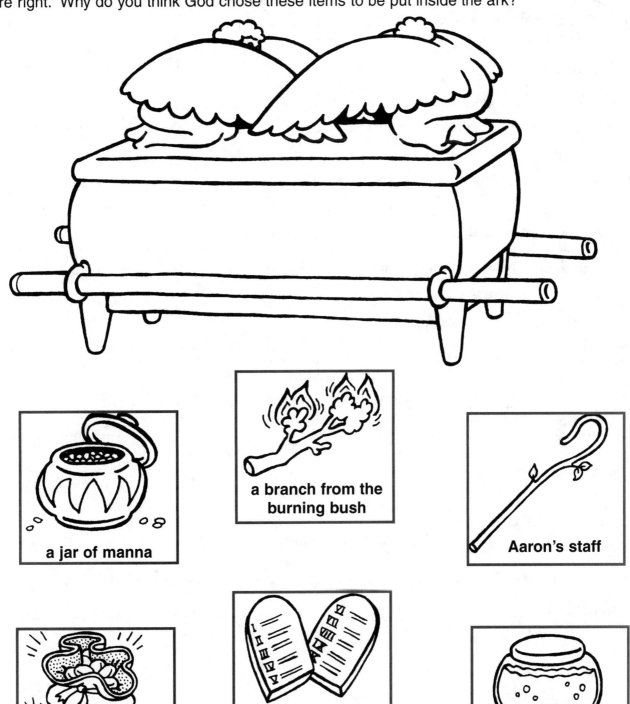

a branch from the burning bush

a jar of manna

Aaron's staff

gold

stone tablets

a jar of water from the Red Sea

Giving to the Lord

Directions: Moses asked the people to give what they had to help build the tabernacle. No one was forced to give, but so many people gave willingly Moses had to ask them to stop because he had far more than he needed for the building! How does God feel about that kind of giving? Look up the Bible verses to find out what God teaches about giving. Then write the underlined words in the song and sing it.

2 Corinthians 9:7

1. Each man should give what he has decided in his _____ to give, not reluctantly or under compulsion, for God loves a _____ giver.

Acts 20:35

2. The Lord Jesus himself said: "It is more blessed to _____ than to _____."

Deuteronomy 15:7b–8, 10

3. Do not be hardhearted or tightfisted toward your poor brother. Rather be openhanded and freely lend him whatever he needs. Give _____ to him and do so without a grudging heart.

Be a Giver

(*Tune:* "She'll Be Comin' 'Round the Mountain")

Are you ____ ____ ____ ____ ____ ____ ____ ____ ____ ____ giving to the Lord?

For God loves a ____ ____ ____ ____ ____ ____ ____ ____ giver, says His Word.

He has given so much to you,

There is only one thing to do—

Open up your ____ ____ ____ ____ ____ and give back to the Lord.

Oh it's better far to ____ ____ ____ ____ than to ____ ____ ____ ____ ____ ____ ____!

Jesus said it and it's what you should believe.

Don't be selfish and unkind;

But just please make up your mind

To share what you have with those who are in need.

Tabernacle Action Rhyme

All God's people brought their offerings–

(*Pretend to carry gifts in your hands or arms.*)

Gold and silver and linen and wood.

(*Count them off on your fingers.*)

They brought so much Moses had to say,

(*Stretch arms out wide.*)

"Stop! That's enough. You've done well!

(*Hold up hand in stop motion; then smile and shake head yes.*)

Then came the workers to use their skills;

(*Walk in place, purposefully.*)

Each one doing his part.

(*Make OK sign with forefinger and thumb.*)

Cutting and sewing and hammering, too,

(*Act out one or all of these activities.*)

Working with all their hearts.

(*Put hand on heart.*)

Moses gave them directions from God

(*Move arms and hands around as if giving directions.*)

As they worked at a strong, steady pace.

(*Pretend to work hard at one of the tasks mentioned above.*)

And when the tabernacle at last was done,

(*Stand back with hands on hips.*)

God's cloud of glory filled the place.

(*Stretch out arms toward heaven.*)

Jesus, Our High Priest

Directions: No one was allowed inside The Most Holy Place of the tabernacle except for the High Priest. He was only permitted to go inside once a year on the Day of Atonement when he went in to ask forgiveness for the sins of the people. Jesus came to Earth to be our High Priest. What did He do for us? To find out, use letters from the number/letter code box to complete the verse. The first letter is done for you. Look up Hebrews 9:12, 28 to check your work.

1	A	D	N	E
2	F	R	T	H
3	L	C	V	I
4	G	O	B	S
	5	**6**	**7**	**8**

JESUS ENTERED THE MOST HOLY PLACE __O__ ____ ____ ____ FOR ALL
                                   4-6   1-7 3-6 1-8

BY HIS OWN ____ ____ ____ ____ ____ , HAVING OBTAINED
           4-7 3-5 4-6 4-6 1-6

____ ____ ____ ____ ____ ____ ____ REDEMPTION. SO CHRIST WAS
1-8 2-7 1-8 2-6 1-7 1-5 3-5

____ ____ ____ ____ ____ ____ ____ ____ ____ ____ ONCE TO TAKE AWAY
4-8 1-5 3-6 2-6 3-8 2-5 3-8 3-6 1-8 1-6

THE ____ ____ ____ ____ OF MANY PEOPLE.
    4-8 3-8 1-7 4-8

What do you think this means?

Moses' Death

(Based on Deuteronomy 31–34)

Moses was born in Egypt and lived there for 40 years. Then he ran to the land of Midian, settled down, got married and had a family, and lived as a shepherd for the next 40 years. When he was 80 years old, God called him to be a prophet and to go back to Egypt and rescue his people. Moses obeyed and led God's people for the next 40 years. When Moses was 120 years old, it was time for a younger prophet to take over and lead the people into the Promised Land. God had chosen Joshua.

Moses and Joshua went to the tabernacle and God appeared to them in a cloud over the entrance. He warned them that the Israelites would continue to be rebellious and unfaithful and one day they would forsake God to worship idols. Most of the people had been so disobedient, God had made them wander in the desert for 40 years until the older generation had died. It was only the younger generation of people who would be allowed to live in the Promised Land. Even Moses would not be able to go into the land because of his disobedience. At Meribah, God had told Moses to speak to a rock and water would come out of it for the people to drink. Moses angrily scolded the people for their complaining, then he hit the rock with his staff. God provided the water as He had promised, but because of Moses' disobedience and because Moses did not give Him the credit for the water, He told Moses he would not be able to enter the Promised Land. (Numbers 20:7–12) However, God graciously allowed Moses to climb Mt. Nebo and look across into the Promised Land.

Before he died, Moses spoke to the Israelites, reminding them of how the Lord had cared for them over the years. "The eternal God is your refuge," he told them, "and underneath are the everlasting arms." (Deuteronomy 33:27) He assured them that God would be with them as they entered the Promised Land and would give them victory over their enemies. Then Moses climbed up Mt. Nebo and God showed him the land He had promised His people. Moses died there on the mountain and God buried him. No one knew where. He was so special the last minutes of his life were spent with God. Though he was 120 years old, Moses' sight was still perfect and his body was still strong.

The Israelites wept and mourned for Moses for a month (the usual time of mourning was seven days); then they listened to their new leader Joshua and did what he said. The Bible tells us that there was never another prophet in Israel like Moses whom the Lord knew face to face. God used him to do amazing miracles and signs in Egypt and during the Israelites' wanderings in the desert. "For no one has ever shown the mighty power or performed the awesome deeds that Moses did in the sight of all Israel." (Deuteronomy 34:12) When God first called him, Moses was hesitant and didn't believe he could be of much use to his people. But God used him to save a nation!

Hundreds of years after his death, Moses made an appearance at Jesus' Transfiguration with Elijah. Jesus talked with them; then suddenly they were gone. What did Moses and Jesus talk about? Perhaps the fact that Jesus was going to save people from slavery, as Moses had, but slavery to sin.

Pictures of Moses' Life

Directions: Look carefully at the pictures of Moses' life. Can you explain what is happening in each picture? Number them from 1 to 6 to show the order in which they happened.

Answer Key

Page 8

1. Amram, Jochebed
2. Drown
3. Three
4. Basket
5. Sister, Miriam
6. Pharaoh's Daughter
7. Moses

Page 10

Page 11

1. Circle around "Moses"
2. Line through "to be called the son of the king of Egypt's daughter"
3. Two lines under "He chose to suffer with God's people"
4. Box around "faith"
5. Dotted line under "all the treasures of Egypt"
6. Three lines under "God's reward"

Page 14

Take off your sandals, for the place where you are standing is holy ground.

Page 15

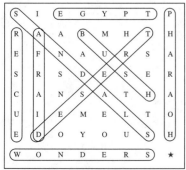

1. bush	4. Egypt	7. desert
2. sandals	5. rescue	8. wonders
3. afraid	6. Pharaoh	

I AM has sent me to you.

Page 17

Drawings of:
Moses' staff becoming a snake
Moses' hand covered with leprosy
The water becoming blood
The signs were to prove to the Jewish leaders that God had sent Moses.

Page 18

1. strength	9. love
2. sing	10. refuge
3. I	11. times
4. morning	12. but
5. fortress	13. will
6. trouble	14. you
7. your	15. are
8. in	16. my

But I will sing of your strength, in the morning I will sing of your love; for you are my fortress, my refuge in times of trouble.

Page 20

J-7 (Hail)

B-9 (Darkness)	H-6 (Boils)	I-5 (Livestock)
F-3 (Gnats)	A-8 (Locusts)	D-2 (Frogs)
G-10 (Sons)	C-1 (Blood)	E-4 (Flies)

Page 22

1. blood	5. flies	9. Egypt
2. locusts	6. signs	10. frogs
3. firstborn	7. hail	11. wonders
4. Ham	8. gnats	12. darkness

death of livestock and boils on people and animals

Answer Key

Page 25

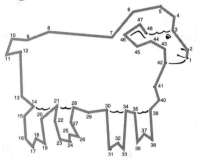

The lamb was killed and its blood was put on the doorposts so God would "pass over" the home. The lamb was then roasted and eaten by the family.

Page 27

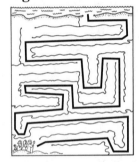

"He saved them for his name's sake, to make his mighty power known."

Page 30

Who among the gods is like you, O Lord? Who is like you—majestic in holiness, awesome in glory, working wonders?

Page 32

planned, free, go, thirst, die, again, meat

Page 37

TRUMPET
LIGHTNING
CLOUD
FIRE
SMOKE
THUNDER
BLAST
TREMBLED

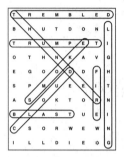

But do not have God speak to us or we will die.

Page 38

1-gods	3-name	5-father, mother
7-adultery	4-holy	10-covet
2-idol	9-false	
6-murder	8-steal	

Page 39

The law was put in charge to lead us to Christ that we might be justified by faith.

Page 41

a jar of manna, Aaron's staff, stone tablets

Page 42

1. heart, cheerful

2. give, receive

3. generously

Song: generously, cheerful, heart, give, receive

Page 44

once, blood, eternal, sacrificed, sins

Page 46

1	5
6	4
2	3